Is Anybody Listening?

Jae-Lynn Snow

India | USA | UK

Presentation by *BookLeaf Publishing*

Web: www.bookleafpub.com

E-mail: info@bookleafpub.com

ISBN: 9789358316155

First edition 2024

To my beautiful daughters! You two are why I go harder!

ACKNOWLEDGEMENT

I wanted to take a chance and share my gift.

PREFACE

For the Geniune Souls.

YOU CAN LEAD A HORSE TO WATER BUT YA ....

Can't make them drink .
Can't make them think.
Gotta watch them sink .
Hope it don't take me.

Break Away.

Can't let you take me .
Won't let you break me .
I just gotta get out and see.
It's about the time to take that leap.

Move Forward.

For the love of the child
Oh my , oh wow
Damn shit got wild
Everything is different now .
I'm in the water , in the deep end .
Know I gotta swim , but I'm sinking .
Was it really worth it in the end?
We just gotta keep on moving .

Freedom

Candles smelling real good
Rolling up this backwood.
Reminiscing on my child hood.
Fought too hard to be understood .
At one point I cared too much ,
NOW if only I could.

If only I could , stand still and breathe .
Take one second just for me .
Right now I choose to believe . . .
Everything happening is meant for me .
Is this what it feels like to be free?

Present Gift.

Forget the past , it doesn't exist .
Forget the future , it doesn't exist.
Live in the present. That's the gift!
The beautiful master piece , given to me. I can
do anything. I gotta get it by any means. Trying
to make sense of reality, but I'm stuck in my
dreams.
Nothing is what it seems.

Hold On.

The only thing constant in the midst of this life is change. How can I maintain? When nothing stays the same. Feel like I'm going insane. Is something wrong with my brain? I don't want to play this game where all I seem to feel is pain. Living this life , what do I have to lose? When I have everything to gain? Deep breaths are all I can take . This ain't it , I gotta make something shake. I'm determined to make a way. Just trust and pray. Everything always ends up okay.

Take 1.

Take, Take a break.
Break , break away.
Just wanna feel safe again.
The emotions are filling , my eyes about to start
spilling
Rise up, I came to win.
Take a deep look of self within.
Go past those shallow depths and hit the deep
end . Hell yes , I can see again. Finally feels like
I can breathe again .

Pause & Celebrate.

Celebrate the grind it took to be able to self create . Celebrate the steps you chose to take . The decisions you chose to make. Cheers to your attempt to make this life great. Your joy and happiness awaits. Hold on tight , the magic is on the way. Live a genuine life everyday. Ignore what "the people" say. Live authentically, spiritually and physically. You can't know what it takes to be me. A small little glimpse is all they will ever see.
Celebrate, you came along way!

Encouragement.

Hey little one , the time has just begun. This one
is for the inner child. I been meaning to say this
for awhile.
Look at you!
My , how you've grown.
You got out here in this world , and you figured
it all out on your own.
Even the things that were unknown.
Not ashamed to learn.
You've finally recognized who you are. Go
ahead baby, you made it through all the scars.
You made it through the rain. You're healing all
your pain . Baby, I'm so glad you came . Came
back to your senses , let me give you some free
game. Don't ever sacrifice yourself for the sake
of love, again. I hope you understand that
boundaries are a real thing. Self love is the best
love, don't let them call you vain.

FOR THE BROKEN HEARTED

I HEAR SHATTERING, DID SOMETHING
BREAK?
THE WINE GLASS? OR WAS THAT THE
WINDOW? LOST LIKE CLUELESS.
THERE'S NO ONE HERE. THERE'S BLOOD
EVERYWHERE. AM I BLEEDING? I FEEL
LIKE SCREAMING. HIGH PITCHED UNTIL
I'M DONE BREATHING. I JUST WANNA
RELEASE THIS STRESS. WHY THIS BITCH
KEEP PUTTING ME TO THE TEST? I FEEL
LIKE SUCH A MESS. WHY AM I GOING
THROUGH THIS?
FEELS LIKE SOMEBODY STABBED ME IN
MY CHEST
HEART FEELS LIKE IT WENT INTO
ELECTRIC SHOCK
MY CHEST IS SO HEAVY
CHEST IS CAVING IN
HERE WE GO, WITH ALL THE LIES
AGAIN! ANXIETY STARTING TO TRIP.
THROAT FULL OF WORDS I CANNOT GET
THEM OUT. WHAT THE HELL WAS ALL OF
THIS ABOUT?

I LOVED TOO HARD , IT LEFT ME
SCARRED.
THIS IS FOR THE BROKEN HEARTED

GASLIGHTING.

12

I'M TIRED OF FIGHTING. I AM TIRED OF
TRYING. EVERYTIME THIS MAN OPEN
HIS MOUTH, I KNOW HE LYING. GOT ME
CRYING. ALL THIS GAS LIGHTING. ALL
THE SHIT I'M FINDING. READY TO DO
SOME TIME MAN. WHEN I SPEAK ON
THE PROBLEM AT HAND, NOW ALL OF A
SUDDEN YOU CAN'T COMPREHEND.
DON'T EVEN WANNA MAKE AMENDS .
ALL YOU GONE DO IS FLIP IT IN THE
END. I JUST WANNA BE ALONE AGAIN!

Resilience.

S/o to Cardi B
I fell down 9 times, but I got up on 10.
I had to learn how to let go, in order for me to
win.
Won't sit up here and pretend , what you see , is
what you get.
Everyday I'm on defense.
Can't let nobody play with my heart again. This
is just the beginning of real healing.

Keep Moving.

As time keeps moving
No time for losing .
Start to make improvements.
Proof myself to no man .
It's ME, I'm choosing!
Just gotta grow through this
Just gotta keep moving .

Ode To My Snows.

Welcome to Motherhood , the best hood . The day finally came , which I knew it would . When I would finally have to hold these little peanuts , it's my job to bring you up into this world , now that's tough. Sometimes I fall short, but you remind me I'm enough. This is a mean world , but you seem to make it sweet . Everything I wasn't before , you made me. You came into my life to TEACH. You made me, become someone I thought couldn't be reached. Thank you for dragging the potential out of me. I strive to be the best mom I can be. I had to get control of my emotions and learn how to sit back and see. Not speak. How to remain calm. How to not enter the spirit of defeat. The GREATEST love , you are my two. If I had to do it all again, I would still choose you. I chose to heal myself, so I wouldn't harm you . My little angels are proof. Proof that magic exists. You girls heal my heart , with every little kiss. A chance to be apart of your life, I wouldn't dare miss this. Serenity & Shiya, you are mommy's bliss.

Decisions.

They asking me to witness, to demonstrate the
act of forgiveness .
I don't think I can do this.
Just do it for the children.
Nothing more, nothing less.
Hell naw, I ain't got time for the stress. Fuck
them, let them stay in distress. I digress.
The people got the most to say , about how I live
my life or how I behave.
Why would I forgive you when you almost put
me in the grave?
Need me to clean your conscience up, well I
ain't the damn maid.
You can try and run but that karma getting paid.
Stop..
I had to do a double take , forgiveness is for
yourself mama , remember you self made.
Free yourself from the mental chains. You can
still place the boundaries you've made.
When you choose forgiveness , you're choosing
to live again.

Black Men Vs Toxicity.

Dear toxic men , I pray you look within . Don't
let the toxicity win. Stop hanging out with ya
ignorant friends . You keep fumbling, so focused
on hustling . Still struggling to be a man . His
mother can't raise him. Only his father can.
Don't get lost between society's rules and free
thought. With some accountability, you can get
far. I just want you to see the king you are. They
don't want you to evolve . They want you to stay
wounded, filled with scars. Stay filled with
sorrows , stop looking forward to tomorrow. If
we can get you out the home , then we have the
control. Where did that little boy's dad go? Now
he about to spiral. Black men you don't even
know what you mean . You don't accept help
from the beautiful black Queens. They really are
afraid to see us act like teams. We could all
benefit from some unity . Did you know you
don't have to stay this way? You survived child
hood , it's time to live okay? I know it was some
people you wish could have stayed. Try healing,
before life has its way.
Self reflect , check that mirror out!
 IT'S NEVER TOO LATE.

Let's work on elevating because the most
dangerous man is educated.

18

For The Black Woman

Dear Black Women
Black women are Goddesses.
Look at that man tryna holla sis.
I know you passionate and curious.
A little shy and mysterious.
Bold and courageous.
Completely full of confidence.
Let's face it.
They tried to make us hate it .
They wanted us to hate on all this, I'm talking
about the racists!
They wanted us to hate our hair , hate our skin,
even hate our men.
Hate who we are, black women , we have came
so far.
Especially dealing with this tough ass life, this
shit is hard!
It would be easier if we could , stop getting
misread and misunderstood. Mistreated , when
are y'all gonna recognize that black women are
needed?
This is not to sound conceited, but this is for my
BLACK GIRLS

HEY! I really mean it! I'm proud of you and I hope all your dreams come true. Keep getting up and kicking ass. That's what real hustlers do. Keep pushing through, keep you a circle of genuine friends who will adjust your crown if they need to.

Thankful.

Woke up feeling great today .
The sun came out to play .
The heat feels so good against my skin.
Allowing me to meditate and zone in.
It's so comforting and warm. Reminding me I
made it through the storms.
As the breeze moves through the trees,
My mind is finally at ease.
I am experiencing peace.

Detaching.

I take a minute and take in everything I see. The beauty that's around me . The beautiful colors leaves no mystery, this world is a canvas and Spirit is an artist . I can't think of one thing to complain about, I'm just glad that I finally made it out. Depression had me in a drought. Took away my smile. I stayed down and remained faithful . I had to trust the unknown . I always believed in miracles.
It ain't over until I say so .
This life is a game yo, gotta play the hand you're dealt though.
I am Thankful for my soul . I had to pay attention , to my own vibration. I had to start speaking my affirmations. I had to start pouring back in , back into myself . Turn my emotional wounds into emotional wealth. Always checking in with my mental health . I had to feel my emotions and release them. I wish everyone the best, even him. This life is temporary and so is everything else. Nothing lasts forever , that's a fact! My alignment came through when I learned how to detach.

Evolution.

23

I no longer dwell , I let go . I can't keep holding
on, If it's not meant for me , then I must move
on . I no longer care about who's right or wrong.
If the connection isn't genuine , please leave me
alone . Finally found home. It was ME all along.
Everything I was in search of , was already
inside of me.
 I had to self reflect and take accountability.
It took some help from up above, for me to tune
in and learn self love.
Forget the past, forget what it was.
Never forget the lessons learned.
I had to focus on my own reality and healing,
now I can tap into my magical spirit .

www.ingramcontent.com/pod-product-compliance
Lightning Source LLC
La Vergne TN
LVHW051248200726
843510LV00011B/1744